CW00404316

THE TEXT-BOOK
OF
JU-JUTSU

As Practised in Japan

*Being a simple treatise on the
Japanese Method of Self Defence*

BY

S. K. UYENISHI

British Library Cataloguing-in-Publication Data
A catalogue record for this book is available from the
British Library

CONTENTS

Sadakazu Uyenishi

Sadakazu Uyenishi was born in 1880, and was amongst the first Japanese jujitsu practitioners to both teach and compete outside of Japan. Uyenishi was born at Osaka Prefecture in Honshu, the main island of Japan. His father, Kichibe Uyenishi, had been a famous athlete, noted for his unusual physical strength and skill at Kenjutsu, horsemanship, swimming and sumo wrestling. As the young Uyenishi was contemplating a military career, his father encouraged him to begin training in jujitsu and enrolled him in a local dojo. He showed considerable skill in his early years, and won several local jujitsu competitions. At the age of twenty, he travelled to London at the invitation of Edward William Barton-Wright, the founder of the eclectic martial art of Bartitsu – and joined his teaching faculty at Shaftesbury Avenue. At the same time, Uyenishi also distinguished himself as a professional wrestler, competing successfully against much larger opponents in contests promoted by Barton-Wright. He quickly gained in popularity and notoriety, and soon established his own dojo, the *School of Japanese Self Defence* at 31 Golden Square, Piccadilly Circus. In 1905, with the assistance of his student E.H. Nelson and writing under his professional wrestling alias of 'Raku', Uyenishi produced his first *Text-Book of Ju-Jutsu*. Although Uyenishi enjoyed life in Edwardian London society; an exotic character whose stylish dress and gentlemanly bearing were considered noteworthy, he returned to Japan in 1908. Little is known of his life after that date, but one biographer placed his death sometime in the run-up to the Second World War. Notable individuals directly influenced by Sadakazu Uyenishi's teaching have included William Garrud, whose book *The Complete Jujitsuan* (published in 1914) became a standard reference work on the subject, and Edith Garrud, who established jujitsu classes for members of the militant Suffragist movement.

PREFACE

It is not without considerable diffidence that I submit this little treatise to the British Public. I have been primarily prompted to do so by a desire to express my appreciation of the great interest, I should, perhaps, say keenness, of those whom I am proud to be able to call not only my pupils but also my friends. This great keenness of theirs has made my work of instruction a real pleasure to me, and has swept aside many of those little troubles which I feared at first might be almost insuperable.

The great consideration which has always been shown to me when I have found it difficult to express myself as clearly as I could wish, owing to my knowledge of English being so small, has given me every incentive to assist my pupils as far as it has been in my power.

With all its incompleteness, and other little shortcomings, for which I crave the indulgence of those who may be so sufficiently interested as to study this little text-book, I launch it on the sea of public opinion, feeling sure that some at least of my old friends will find it useful. If it in any way helps to bring Ju-Jutsu into a more prominent position among English Athletic Sports (and this I may say appears to me to be a matter of supreme and even of National Importance) I shall then be able to feel that my labours have not been altogether in vain.

The Army authorities have included the science in the curriculum of their Gymnasia. The Police have adopted many tricks, locks, holds, and throws from Ju-jutsu and have included these in their system of training. In short, so many people are beginning to realise that an acquaintance with the "soft art" would form no mean addition to their general knowledge, that I have felt that this little book of mine will not be an entirely superfluous effort.

I have endeavoured to explain, as clearly as possible, the preliminary stages of the science, so that the reader may be enabled, at all events, to graduate himself in the art, and, after subsequent practice, obtain a fair amount of proficiency. If I have not been successful in fully carrying out this ambition, I trust that I may have so far interested you in Ju-jutsu, that you will be tempted to make its closer acquaintance. And, should I have succeeded in this, I can assure you that I shall have rendered you no mean service.

Should any of you feel at all disposed to tender me any thanks for my services, I trust that you will transfer these to those of my friends and pupils (and I would here specially wish to mention Mr. E. H. Nelson) who have so kindly assisted me in the preparation and arrangement of the photographs and matter, and also to Messrs. Gaumont et Cie. for their very excellent cinematograph pictures of the various movements.

THE TEXT BOOK
OF
JU-JUTSU

as

Practised in Japan

CHAPTER I

INTRODUCTION

It is said that Ju-jutsu was first practised some 2,000 years ago. If this is correct then it must be far and away the oldest exercise in the world, and one which has been continuously practised. But without going into the question of its origin, I may mention that it was practised by the *Samurai*, or fighting men of Old Japan, for many centuries, and that until the last fifty years no one outside the warrior caste was ever initiated into its mysteries. But with the passing away of the old order of things together with the Shogun, and the dawning of the new era of *Meiji* (or enlightened government), the *Samurai* ceased to be a caste apart and gave to their country not only their own priceless services, but also all their store of knowledge in the science of physical well-being and self-defence.

The value of Ju-jutsu was immediately recognised by the Government and people, who adopted it with such enthusiasm that it has now become almost an integral part of the life of the majority of the nation. It forms an extensive department of the naval, military, and police training, proficiency in the science being almost an essential preliminary to promotion.

Ju-jutsu, therefore, had the *imprimatur* of the Japanese Government, and I do not think that I can be accused of ultra-patriotism, when I claim that this evidence of its worth should be adequate testimonial to all who may desire one. The Mikado's Government was not in the habit of wasting either their own or their people's time!

The word Ju-jutsu itself has been variously translated into English, and perhaps I should add American, as meaning "muscle-breaking," "the excellent secret art," "the art of softness," or "the gentle art," but it is quite impossible to convey in one or two descriptive words of this sort what Ju-jutsu really is.

Perhaps it may not be without interest if I make here a slight digression and refer to a few somewhat analogous styles of self-defence, which are either now, or were formerly in vogue in Japan, most of which styles are more or less related to Ju-jutsu, being either branchings off from that science, or originally distinct systems from which the modern Judo, or Ju-jutsu, has been compounded. *Judo* may be roughly translated as "the soft way," as Ju-jutsu is anglicised into "the soft art," in opposition to *Kendo* or *Ken-jutsu*, "the hard way" and "the hard art" respectively. This last mentioned style of self-defence is the elaboration of the old two-sword play of the *samurai* or "two-sworded men." And here the reader will probably grasp the inner truth of Ju-jutsu, the victor establishing the superiority of leverage and balance, two soft, delicate qualities, over the harder, rougher ones of strength and force.

One of the styles alluded to, known as the *Kempo*, which may be roughly described as a method of killing people, possessed many points of resemblance to Ju-jutsu but was totally different in practice, being a system of self-defence against sudden attack with intent to kill and replying thereto in kind. It was certainly more closely related to Ju-jutsu than are Boxing (even under the old Prize Ring rules) or *le savate* to Wrestling. It might perhaps be best compared to that very strenuous old Greek Physical Contest, which was known as the *Pancration*. By-the-way, I may here remark on the possible derivation of the old English phrase "Kempery man" and the Anglo-Saxon *cempa*, signifying "a warrior," from the Japanese *Kempo*. This is a point which should not be without interest to etymologists, and particularly to those who follow the late Professor Max Muller in his theory of the Indo-Germanic origin of the Anglo-Saxon Race.

Kempo, of course, was a system of attack and defence which branched off from Ju-jutsu into the paths of strenuous endeavour, but, apart from the fact that it was less scientific than Ju-jutsu, it was declared an illegal practice when the sanctity of human life was recognised under the new regime.

Another analogous system, known as *tori* in some parts of Japan and as *shime* in others, was an extension of Ju-jutsu in the department of ground work, and it is more than possible that many of the locks and holds of Ju-jutsu were originated

9

by exponents of *tori*. The last-named system cannot, however, be compared with the "soft art" as a method of self-defence, as but slight importance was devoted to "throws," the *modus operandi* being mainly confined to falling to the ground yourself and then pulling your opponent down, there to struggle for the victorious lock.

I do not wish to imply that the power to dislocate a joint, break a limb, or even to kill an opponent, which were the cause of the prohibition of *Kempo*, do not exist in Ju-jutsu (since all experts are well acquainted with them), but it will be as well to point out that these powers are rarely, if ever, exercised. The locks are so complete in themselves that the mere *threat* of damage which their application implies, is sufficient to induce even the most obstinate opponent to cry for quarter.

It may perhaps be urged against Ju-jutsu that, among exponents who were lacking in the spirit of true sportsmanship, limbs might frequently be broken or dislocated, but I always remind such critics that even in rough mining and other districts, where everyone carries "a gun," people are generally particularly careful to play "the game" (whatever it may be) strictly according to the rules.

I will venture to claim for Ju-jutsu that it is not only the finest system of self-defence extant, but that it is also second to none as a system of Physical Culture, being unrivalled as a means of developing rapidity of movement, and perfect balance, and furthermore is certainly not to be despised as a means of developing strength and muscle of the right quality. Then again, it is a magnificent sport, game, or exercise, call it what you will, second to none in the mental, moral and physical qualities which it calls into play, and certainly superior to every other with which I am acquainted in that it is never monotonous or uninteresting either to the performer or spectator.

"Of the making of books there is no end, and much study may be a weariness to the flesh," perhaps, but I do not believe that this treatise will altogether deserve the latter stricture, if it serves to correct some of the misconceptions in the public mind that have been instilled therein by several books which have recently appeared, professing to give instruction in the whole art of Ju-jutsu. Consider, for instance, the various exercises which have been alleged to be essential preliminaries to Ju-jutsu training. Well, I have never seen any Ju-jutsuan who ever practised them. In the old style of Ju-jutsu before my time, there was I believe an exercise called the *tai atari* or "toughing" exercise, in which the practitioners rushed at each other, chest to chest, somewhat in the style of the exercise called *dzu-dzu-Ki*, practised by the *Sumo* wrestlers, who develop their strength and hardiness by *butting* each other. In fact, all these "resistance" movements, concerning which certain pseudo authorities on Ju-jutsu have been so fluent, would, if of any practical value at all, be more suitable as training for the *Sumo* style of wrestling than for Ju-jutsu. For

11

Sumo is contested by big heavy men, often standing about six feet in height and weighing from eighteen to twenty stone, who rely almost entirely on their strength and avoirdupois to give them the victory, not that they are without various tricks, holds and moves of their own.

Such training as the Ju-jutsu novice does indulge in is taught in the schools in Japan, and is styled the *taiso-no-kata*, or physical culture exercise for boys and girls, comprising *go-no-kata*, which means "muscle development for strength," and *ju-no-kata*, or "soft exercise,"—preparation in suppleness and agility.

These form the whole groundwork training for the various branches which may be described as *Ji-jutsu*, or balance and throws; *tai-jutsu*, literally "strong style," implying the use of strength; and the *Judo* style (as *Ju-jutsu* proper is often styled) which does not imply so much ground work as was practised in earlier times.

Then, again, it is quite erroneous to suppose that any special diet is essential to Ju-jutsu training. I have been greatly amused at some extraordinary statements on this topic contained in the books referred to above. For instance, water-drinking is mentioned as though it were a panacea for all evils and a practice to which all Ju-jutsuans were excessively addicted. Of course, water is a more suitable beverage than *sake*, or beer, for a Ju-jutsuan, as it is for all athletes, but I certainly do not recommend anyone to drink even water frequently or copiously immediately before or after a contest. At least twenty minutes to half-an-hour should elapse after a bout, before water should be taken.

With regard to bathing, you should of course bathe at least once a day, and may even, if you are so minded, have as many as three each day during training, but that number should not be exceeded.

In the matter of eating, it is unnecessary to retail the diet adhered to in Japan, as I cannot see that it has any influence one way or the other on Ju-jutsu training. As in all athletic training, plain food eaten in moderation and according to taste, will be found best. The same may be said on the subject of smoking. Excessive use of tobacco in any form is, of course, injurious to health, but were a contestant to indulge in a cigarette immediately before a contest, it would not occasion any remark. I can assure you that there are no cranks among us.

I am afraid that this Introductory chapter seems to be spreading itself out to a length which I scarcely contemplated, but I have felt that, before proceeding to tell you what Ju-jutsu really *is*, I must at least mention a few of the things which it is *not*. And these, I regret to have to say, include the majority of those marvellous powers, etc., which are and have been so mysteriously referred to in most recent publications in Ju-jutsu.

I propose to put simply before the reader, clear definitions and descriptions of the various falls, throws, and locks which are used in actual Ju-jutsu contests. The "pinches" to which reference is so often made, are not only no longer used, but are not even *permitted* in any Ju-jutsu contests at any of the important meetings held in Japan. I am afraid that any man who depended on one of these "pinches" in order to secure a victory in a serious contest would find himself sadly disappointed. These "pinches" are absolutely barred, together with hitting, finger gripping, and twisting or using the hand on an opponent's face, or similar movements and tricks whereby damage might be caused before the signal of defeat could be given.

In fact so much care has been devoted to the preservation of the purely sporting element of Ju-jutsu, that I venture to claim among its other virtues that of being the least dangerous to life and limb of any sport or contest in existence.

For self-defence against sudden and ruffianly attack. however, the more dangerous movements might be utilised in case of necessity, and I think one could scarcely be blamed for doing pretty serious damage to any hooligan who might attack one.

Now that modern conditions have so widened the field of female occupation, and have, in consequence, necessitated their frequently going to and from their work unescorted, it would be of great advantage were Ju-jutsu made a special feature of a young lady's education.

We should not then hear of those cases of assault and robbery to which many young ladies are so frequently subject. I have taught many young English ladies a dozen or so tricks of defence, which have rendered them secure against any danger resulting from ruffianly attack, and am personally acquainted with many instances in which several of my pupils have been thus enabled easily to defeat attacks from ruffians who would have proved formidable handfuls even to the burliest policeman.

It would be impossible, within the limits of this work, to explain fully the *whole* science of Ju-jutsu, so I have sought rather in this volume to confine myself to as descriptive an account as possible of the principal breakfalls, throws, and locks, which will enable the student to ground himself thoroughly for the game. I have endeavoured so to express myself that most of you will be able to teach yourselves, and be fitted to combat on fairly equal terms any but the most skilled and experienced opponents.

The *Kata* and ground work need such full and careful explanation that I propose to leave this to a future volume in which they can be fully dealt with, and in which I shall have space also to go into advanced tricks of combat and display.

The eleven throws and eight locks with which I have dealt are those most in use, and I trust that my explanations and the cinematographic illustrations will enable you to master them fully.

Before proceeding to special descriptions I will, with your leave, indulge in a few more or less necessary preliminary instructions and words of caution.

For the necessary costume all that is really needed is a rough stout jacket and a pair of bathing drawers. The jacket can be of any stout material, but, if you propose going in for extensive practice, you will find the real Ju-jutsu jackets, made in Japan, which will cost you about a guinea each, the cheapest in the long run, as they will stand an almost incalculable amount of wear. But for a beginner any old stout jacket, fastened by a sash, will serve.

The Ju-jutsu mats as made in Japan, also form the most suitable floor covering, but any matting, provided it be thick enough and not too rough, will serve, while an ordinary grass plot of course will form an ideal scene either for practice or encounter.

When engaging an opponent take hold of him in a light grip with both hands. It is also advisable to take hold of him at points slightly below the level of his shoulders, as this will enable you to give him a stronger pull. Choose also points as far apart as possible in order to obtain the fullest amount of leverage. Then, in order that you may be able to *swing* your opponent bodily if necessary, it is best to hold him by the collar with one hand and by the sleeve with the other.

In the special instructions to each throw or lock, I have, for the sake of clearness, written "hold your opponent by the

16

collar with your left hand, and by his left sleeve with your right; step back with your left foot," etc., etc.: but I do not thereby wish you to take these instructions as being arbitrary ones. The holds may be reversed or adapted to suit the students' own physical peculiarities. I will not even suggest that my way is the best way. Nearly every man is suppler or more active in some one direction than in others, and he will therefore find that he can work more effectively in certain directions opposite to those which I have suggested as being those best adapted to a right-handed man. But he will not do well always to confine himself to his own strong points in this particular; he must remember that his opponent may also have strong points as well as weak ones, and that a study of these last will well repay him. Then again, since great success at Ju-jutsu can only fall to those possessed of all-round suppleness, agility, and activity it is not advisable to develop only your strong points and neglect your weak ones. Rather cultivate the weak points and practise every pull, lock, or movement with *both* feet, *both* hands, and in every possible direction, so as to be prepared to meet every class of opponent.

FINAL WORDS OF CAUTION

Before proceeding to the description of the various throws, locks, etc., I feel it very necessary to draw particular attention to the fact that, if the student be unable to procure the assistance of a competent instructor, he should exercise the utmost caution when trying any of the falls, throws, or locks, as many of them are sufficiently severe to cause serious damage if attempted in a rough or careless manner.

It must always be borne in mind that the whole fabric of Ju-jutsu is based on the utilisation of strategy, agility and rapidity of movement, rather than on strength pure and simple.

Success is achieved rather by the conservation of energy than by the use of it.

There is a proverb to the effect that "Knowledge is power," and knowledge at Ju-jutsu is the beginning and end of power. Any man fully equipped with a practical knowledge of it need have but little fear of any opponent not similarly equipped however formidable the other may be in weight, height, and strength. You can really never know too much, or even enough, about Ju-jutsu. For almost every time you engage with an opponent who is at all your equal you will find that he has something to teach you, or even supposing that you can learn nothing from him, you will probably discover something for yourself; most probably some quicker method of carrying out a movement. It must always be borne in mind that lightning rapidity of action is the keynote of success in Ju-jutsu.

S. K. U.

THE BUDOKWAI

The Budokwai, founded in 1918 by G. Koizumi, Esq., at 15 Lower Grosvenor Place, is an amateur Society conducted by honorary effort. The essence of its work is to spread the Japanese form of culture known as Judo (Ju-Jutsu) such that its growth shall be dignified, free from professionalism, and permanent.

The Society has given in London and other parts of the country many displays, the idea of which has been to educate the public as to the true nature of Judo, and not to provide the Western sports 'fan' with entertainment.

The Society held annually its own display which served as a public record of its yearly progress.

CHAPTER II

BALANCE

Nearly everyone, I suppose, has some knowledge of balance; or at least they know what the word means. But I think I may safely say that very few, if any, have given even a passing thought to it as applied to their own bodies. I may therefore be pardoned for starting right at the beginning.

The human body, as everyone knows, is (or should be) carried erect on two legs, and the reason for this must be apparent to anyone who will ask himself the question why. The reason is simply because, in the first place, it is better balanced, and secondly, because the balance is more easily *maintained* in the erect position.

Walking consists of leaning forward or *losing* the balance in a forward direction, when a leg is brought forward to *catch* the *balance* again. In walking backwards we have the same process reversed. Now suppose a man starts to walk backwards and tries to step out to the front after losing his balance, no matter how slightly, in the backward direction, we find that unless a leg is quickly brought back to help him regain his equilibrium, he falls, no matter how *strong be may be*, and it is on this simple scientific fact that the whole fabric of Ju-jutsu is based, as far as what may be called the standing part is concerned.

And I may say right here that it is the quick and agile man who will have the ability to regain balance more easily after having once lost it, and not the strong man, for strength pure and simple can in no way be brought forward as a factor in balance.

Knowledge of balance, and how to disturb it, is the "mystery" which enables the Ju-jutsu man so easily to throw stronger and heavier opponents without any great effort or without using strength (in the common acceptation of the term).

For the information of those who may think that great strength is necessary, or even an advantage, I should like to remind them (as many perhaps are not prone to reason things out for themselves) that if you are weighing even tons of material on a *scale* or *balance*, a single ounce or the lightest touch of even a single finger will move the beam down at a certain *point of balance*.

In the same way, if the human body is at a certain point of balance, the least little pull or push will disturb that balance, and a fall becomes inevitable *unless* support is adjusted at or before the critical moment.

There must of course be a moment after which it becomes physically impossible to readjust the lost balance, or in other words, to "save the fall." It will be evident, even to those who may be most sceptical at first, that no amount of strength exerted after that point has been reached will be of the least avail; so that it is after all only a matter of common-sense to say that on a point of actual balance strong and weak are on a par.

This will become most apparent in actual practice to the novice when he is first successful in making, say, a clean ankle throw. For a moment he will scarcely realise that he has made the throw, and will feel rather that his adversary fell on purpose, but after a few more successes he will understand that if the correct or psychological moment has been utilised, the amount of exertion which he has actually used has been so trifling that it could scarcely be definable as "strength," as strength is generally understood. However, the student must not misunderstand me on this point and think that he need put little if any force into his "pulls." These must be definite and sharp and executed at the precise psychological moment, as described hereafter in the pages dealing with the various throws.

Primarily, when the student is acting on the defensive and as he is trying to avoid being thrown by any or every trip or trick which can be brought into play against him, he must *at all times* endeavour to hold himself in perfect balance, the position best adapted for this being the one which nature intended us to assume, namely the one I have already mentioned, an easy, upright, or perfectly erect position.

Balance is the whole secret of Ju-jutsu both for attack and defence, and cannot be too assiduously practised. The student must *continually* bear it in mind, as a momentary omission will place him immediately at the mercy of any opponent who has any practical knowledge of Ju-jutsu.

The next thing to remember is that all movements, and especially every step taken either forward or backward, should be performed in the most natural, easy manner possible, at an expenditure of the least possible amount of exertion. There should be no stiffness or prolonged muscle tension whatever, either in legs, arms, or body. The hips should be perfectly loose, or perhaps it would be more correct to say that the trunk itself should be held quite loosely. Those of you who go in for horse riding will, perhaps, more readily grasp my meaning and I can find nothing so appropriate with which to compare the carriage of the body necessary for Ju-jutsu, as the easy, graceful "seat" of the "natural" horseman.

Too much stress cannot be laid on this point since it is perhaps the *most* important of all, certainly quite as important as the maintenance of perfect balance. The *whole* body should be perfectly supple, so that when any movement is necessary, it may be made with the least possible preliminary fatigue or delay. For it takes time to relax and contract muscles; with some people this operation takes longer than with others, so that if both movements have to be made, valuable time will be lost.

For instance, suppose you wish to throw your opponent with, say, the ankle throw (hereinafter described) to the right.

In order to do so you must pull with your right hand. This should be done with a sudden sharp jerk and not with a long, strong, slow pull. It will be as well to explain the reason for this now, so that the student may appreciate the advantage of keeping such a very small detail in his mind.

In the first place, a sudden sharp jerk requires less expenditure of energy, and the muscles do not get tired so quickly as they would if a prolonged strain were put on them, while secondly, the sudden pull does not disturb your own balance as much as the long pull would, which is a most important point.

For example, when you wish to pull something or someone towards you, you naturally hang back and so lose your balance in a backward direction just sufficiently (if you can gauge it correctly) to compensate the pull. So that on the completion of the pull you will have regained your balance.

Now the nearer you can keep your body to the actual balancing point, or correct balance, the more difficult it will be to *throw* you, or in the case of an attempted throw, the greater chance will you have to recover and so save yourself from disaster. You will therefore understand that the method, otherwise effective, which will entail the least deviation from this balancing point is not only the safest, but also the best.

At this point I may as well explain why your whole

body should not be kept rigid, but, on the contrary, as free from strain as possible. If rigid you are more easily thrown, particularly if you are a victim of pernicious systems of Physical Culture which cause abnormal development, bordering on the condition known as muscle-bound, as I find so many strong men are. This generally makes them stiff, as well as slow and cumbrous in movement, and consequently longer in making the effort to regain the lost balance. Then again, a greater amount of leverage is obtained by keeping your body supple and lissom, and last but by no means least, it hurts far more to fall stiffly than easily. (See Chapter on Breakfall.)

As before advised, always walk as naturally as possible, *don't cross your legs*, but rather keep them slightly apart.

Particular care should be taken on this point when you are being swung round, as by failing to preserve a proper distance between your feet, you will present your opponent with the opportunity for an easy throw, especially if your legs be crossed.

The human biped was constructed to move mainly in a forward direction. Moving backwards is rather more difficult. But sideways is quite out of the question as far as ease, grace, or comfort is concerned, and knowing this, the Ju-jutsu expert quickly takes advantage of any opportunity that offers to make any of the throws that have been designed to meet and are particularly suited to such movements.

One of the principal mistakes which the novice makes during

his first few lessons is the perhaps not altogether unnatural trick he has of keeping the arms straight out in front when holding his opponent, in an attempt to "keep him off." Since this leads to resistance and consequently flexed muscles, it is a serious fault and one that might even prove a dangerous one in serious combat, as the arms are far more likely to be broken or dislocated when straightened than when they are bent. Both arms should be limp, and the grip on your opponent's coat a loose one, so that it may be instantly tightened for a throw or as quickly released when circumstances require it.

Don't resist when your opponent pushes you; rather, increase your pace in that direction and pull him a little at the same time, or vice versa should he pull you. *Don't* let him ever get the "strain" on you, but go with him, if anything a little faster than his pull would cause you to. By following this precept you are—if I may describe it so—almost catching your balance before he makes you lose it, while he is practically losing his and is without the aid of your resistance—on which he has been more or less depending, to help him regain *his* balance. Thus, in an easy and simple manner, you neutralise his efforts to get you off your balance and at the same time create a favourable opportunity of effecting a throw, by keeping him off his.

Personally, I may say that, on occasions, I have found it a comparatively easy matter, even when wrestling with men who have won their laurels at European styles of wrestling, to throw them off their feet by a simple pull on the collar and sleeve when they are standing in the ordinary bent body or leaning forward position usually adopted by Catch-as-catch-can or Græco-Roman wrestlers. They press forward to such an extent, that their bodies assume a position in which, if they were not supported by me, they would fall down without any assistance, so that under such circumstances it should not be difficult to understand that a little tug in the direction in which they are pushing is quite sufficient to cause a fall. At the same time they lay themselves open to many other throws, particularly the one known as the stomach throw, a picturesque and singularly effective throw, and one which even a slender girl can use against the burliest opponent if she has once properly learnt it.

CHAPTER III

BREAKFALL

(*Ha-uchi*, how to fall without hurting yourself.)

The word Ha-uchi is composed of the two Japanese words, *Hane* (a wing) and *utsu* (to strike). In ordinary parlance it is applied to the wing flapping a bird often indulges in, not in actual flight, but such as may be frequently observed in a farmyard when a rooster crows; or, as some may have noticed, the peculiar "drumming" with the wings that some birds use to call their mates.

In practising some of the methods of breaking the force of a fall, the resemblance of the flapping wings to the beating arms will doubtless suggest itself to the reader.

THE ART OF FALLING

After some little practice in the proper method of walking, and having thereby attained some knowledge of the art of balance, the student should make up his mind to learn how to fall properly.

No amount of theoretical knowledge will enable a student to accomplish this. Actual practice is absolutely necessary. The natural tendency to put out the hand, or hands, in the direction in which one is falling, must be overcome, for this habit absolutely invites a sprained wrist or a bruised arm. The Ju-jutsu method is a remarkably simple one, yet, incredible as it may seem to the uninitiated, wonderfully effective.

In watching the practice of Ju-jutsu for the first time, the novice will doubtless wonder how it is that, in spite of the resounding bang which he hears when a fall is effected, no damage or inconvenience is suffered by the victim, and he is surprised to see him rise briskly to his feet and proceed with his practice as though nothing untoward had occurred.

The explanation is simple enough. The bang he hears when a man is thrown is not the thud of the body striking the ground, as might naturally be supposed, but the properly timed blow of an arm or a leg as it breaks the fall by striking the mat.

The striking or beating of the mat should be made with a straight outstretched arm, and a fraction of a second before the body reaches the ground. If this is properly done, the impact of arm and body *appear* simultaneous.

If the blow with the arm, which it is most important to note *must* be straight, is sufficiently strong and in the right place, not only is the fall an absolutely harmless one, but even the resulting shock of the body striking the ground is practically unnoticeable.

There are several methods of practising the falls and I would strongly advise students in their preliminary attempts at least, to arrange something soft to fall on, as mistakes are sure to be made, no matter how carefully directions may be followed. It will be best to deal with each method singly, and it may be as well to state that the cinematographic illustrations were taken at the rate of about 40 per second, thus showing every gradation of each movement. The pictures themselves will be found as informative as the description.

FIRST BREAKFALL

(SITTING)

The beginner need have no fear of practising the first method of falling properly, and before describing this, I would like to sound a note of warning to those who may think it unnecessary to start with such simple preliminaries. If they will only take the trouble to try this method a few times it will, in all probability, save them many a nasty jar that they may suffer if they omit to do so.

First, start in a sitting posture on the ground, with the chin well in; bring both hands forward, arms extended, the feet drawn up, in a position somewhat similar to that of an oarsman about to dip his oar; roll quietly over on to the back (as the oarsman might if he "caught a crab") and, just before the shoulders reach the ground, beat out to the sides with both the arms still extended, striking the ground with the whole of the arm held from the tips of the fingers to the shoulders, at an angle of about 45 degrees to the body. To continue, straighten the legs for a moment and swing the body up to the sitting position again, when another roll backwards can be made and the beat continued as at first.

By practising this for a few minutes, it will soon be found that, if the feet are drawn in quickly as the sitting posture is regained, the whole of the weight of the body may be easily caught on the feet, so that one could stand erect in a moment by straightening the legs; but don't do this at once.

Continue rolling back and striking the ground and return to the feet again, straightening the legs a little more every time until you get fairly on to the feet, so that at last you will experience no difficulty in starting from a standing position, bending the legs till the squatting position is reached, rolling over backwards and beating the ground, all in one continuous motion.

When this is thoroughly mastered, no difficulty should be found in the second step.

FIRST BREAKFALL "A"

FIRST BREAKFALL "B"

SECOND BREAKFALL

THIRD BREAKFALL

SECOND BREAKFALL

(ONE HAND)

Stand erect on both feet. Raise the *left foot* off the ground with the leg straight, then, by bending the *right* leg, sink slowly down as if about to sit on the ground as near as possible to the right heel, precisely as in the preceding method, save that you are on one foot instead of both.

During this movement, the right hand should be raised from the side, with the arm straight, or it may be slightly bent towards the left, so as to be ready to strike the mat; then just as the body rolls backwards and before the back actually touches the ground, a sharp blow should be delivered to the right, at a point half way between the angle formed by the body and the arm were it stretched out horizontally (or in a line with the shoulders).

In other words, if the blow has been properly delivered, the student should find, when he is lying flat on his back, that his right arm forms an angle of about 45 degrees with his right leg.

It must be borne in mind that the blow should be a strong one, the whole, or as much of the whole length of the arm as is possible from the tips of the fingers to the shoulder, striking the mat.

The accompanying illustration will show this breakfall in actual use after a throw. As will be seen, when in actual practice much of the *weight* of the fall is taken off, both by the "thrown" man's hold on his opponent and also by his opponent's hold on him.

A simple pat or slap with the hand, with the arm bent, is quite ineffective, and particular care should be always taken that the arm is straight when the blow is struck, for otherwise a bruised elbow or damaged shoulder may be the result.

Now all this may seem very complicated on paper, but with the assistance of the illustrations, the student should have no difficulty in following out the directions given, or in mastering them in detail.

It is perhaps unnecessary to mention that this method is well worth the trouble needed to acquire it, for when the pupil is thrown in the course of ordinary practice he will, provided he knows how to "break fall" properly, be under no apprehension of receiving an uncomfortable jar, but will be immediately ready to spring to his feet and proceed with the bout; while under more serious circumstances than a friendly practice, he will be at once prepared to meet attack in whatever form it may come, and possibly even to make such a speedy recovery as to take his assailant quite unawares and turn what may have appeared a defeat into signal success.

FAULTS TO AVOID

It may be useful to those who desire to learn, to know some of the faults frequently made by beginners.

Some start by sitting down with both legs straight, or forget to beat. Some beat too late. Others put the arm straight out behind, or to the side, and don't beat at all, or else fall with the arm bent, at the elbow, sometimes beating a light blow with the hand, but as often as not omitting the blow altogether.

These are the main points to be avoided, and too much care cannot be taken to see that they are avoided. Most of my pupils, however, have managed to pick up the idea quite easily after a few lessons, and I am sure some of them are quite surprised to find that they are not only enabled to strike the blow at the right moment, but that getting the arm at the most effective angle with the body becomes entirely automatic.

IN EXPLANATION

Perhaps a little illustration may make it clearer how such a simple thing as a blow with the arm or leg, as the case may be, should be effective, as it undoubtedly is, in breaking a fall.

We will suppose that a good swinging blow with the arm will register somewhere between 200 and 600 lbs. pressure. I think this is well within the limit when we consider that a blow with the fist will develop anything up to 2,000 lbs.

The weight of the ordinary man we will put at 10 to 11 stone, say, 150 lbs. Now, if the force developed at the point of impact owing to the height of the fall reaches two, or even three or four times the original weight of the body, then nearly, if not quite, all the shock of impact is taken up by the blow struck prior to the time that the body reaches the ground; consequently the balance of shock, if any, that the body receives, only amounts to a few odd pounds which would be only equivalent to a mild pat on the back.

Or, to put it in another way, if the force of the blow takes up three-quarters of the force of a body falling a specified distance, say, two feet, then the actual remaining distance of the fall left over would only be about, say, six inches, which would not be a very serious matter compared with an unbroken fall from the original height named.

Of course these figures are only suggested and may be quite a long way out, but if so, I feel sure that they err on the safe side.

The same remark holds good in regard to the suggested distance of the fall, as a sheer fall of two feet from the ground is seldom likely to occur; one foot or some portion of the body will be on the ground all the time, or will at least reach it some time before the rest of the body arrives. And besides this, the support from the hold on one's assailant, or vice versa, would very greatly minimise the speed of fall, when the force of impact would of necessity be less.

THIRD BREAKFALL

(ON BACK, ALTERNATE)

Another method of practising the beat is to lie flat on the back, raise the right hand upwards and slightly across the body to the left, so that a good deal of swing power may be put into the blow, and at the same time raise the left foot off the ground, with the knee bent.

Now make a simultaneous stroke with the left foot and right hand, so that it would seem as if only one blow had been given.

Twist the body slightly to the right side and bring the left hand up and slightly across to the right side.

If this has been properly done, the momentum gained should enable one to rest for a fraction of a second on the right arm and left foot while the right foot is being raised; then, when falling back again, the blow is delivered with the left hand and right foot and repeated alternately.

A little schooling of this sort soon enables the pupil to strike a simultaneous blow with foot and hand which is often of considerable assistance in some of the throws.

In this, as in the former method, the blow should be

delivered with the hand and arm straight and at an angle of 45 degrees with the body.

For Illustration see facing page 35.

FOURTH BREAKFALL

(HEAD OVER HEELS)

There is a somewhat simple acrobatic feat, frequently performed by children of tender years and commonly known as "Head-over-Heels," which, from the spectators' point of view, resembles another form of the "Breakfall."

Though apparently similar, it is actually a very different thing, for whereas in the "Head-over-heels" the main force of the fall is taken by the back, the spine coming in direct contact with the ground, in Ha-uchi it does not or should never do so, the impact being taken up by the beat of the arm and leg.

One or two of the throws, such as *Sutemi* or *Yoko-Sutemi*, which are commonly practised by the more advanced students, frequently give one an opportunity to save oneself in this manner, and the ability to do so is of great value. In addition to this it makes a very neat, I might almost say ornamental, finish to what in the ordinary way would be an awkward and perhaps rather heavy tumble, the one who falls regaining his feet immediately with one continual movement.

FOURTH BREAKFALL "HEAD-OVER-HEELS"

42

The student should stand with both feet together, bent forward, placing the right hand on the mat, the left forearm with the left hand pointing across and directly towards the right hand.

When in this position, with the head bent slightly to the right, he must push off with both feet, precisely as if he were about to turn the ordinary "Head-over-heels," but, while rolling forward, the body should be given a slight twist to the right, so that the outside of the right leg from the thigh to the ankle strikes the mat.

The left leg is brought slightly forward or across the right, so that the sole of the left foot also strikes the ground both legs being kept straight, but in rapid action this is not absolutely necessary, as will be seen by the position of my left leg in the illustration.

At the same moment, the right arm from the tips of the fingers to the shoulder should beat the mat a strong blow in the usual "Breakfall manner." This arm must also be straight.

The foregoing is the method in which the student should practise this at first, but when he has become more adept, he may follow my movements exactly as shown in the cinematographic illustration, in which he will note that I have not brought my left leg in front of my right. I have kept this behind and, as shown in the picture, slightly bent, this being more or less necessary to assist in regaining an upright position.

FIFTH BREAKFALL

(THE STRAIGHT BACK)

There are two more falls by which the efficacy of the *ha-uchi* method is admirably evidenced, but it would be unwise for the beginner to attempt them.

If, however, he attains proficiency in the methods already described and realises from practical experience the value of beating the mat—he may then make the experiment, if he cares to, beginning very cautiously.

But I would like to state that I would not advise his doing so, save under the guidance of a competent instructor.

. . . . . .

For the first of these falls, the straight back, stand erect with the feet together, bending the leg meanwhile (as near the mat as possible, at first); then lean back and, just as the balance is lost, jump so as to land flat on the back. While falling, the hands, palms to the rear, and arms straight, should be brought forward, so that before actually reaching the ground, both arms are enabled to strike vigorous blows about twelve inches from the body, directly backwards, or, in other words, immediately prior to the moment the body reaches the ground, directly downwards.

The position of the hands when striking the mat, should be close to the spot where the thighs would be had the legs been straight, but about twelve inches away from the body.

FIFTH BREAKFALL "THE STRAIGHT BACK"

45

Photo by L. Gaumont et Cie

THE SIXTH BREAKFALL OR "JUMP INTO SPACE"

46

SIXTH BREAKFALL

(JUMP INTO SPACE)

The third cinematographic series illustrates a fair example of what may be done in the way of "breaking-fall."

The photographs clearly show a couple of rapid steps forward, a spring upwards and forwards as high as a man's shoulders, and a flat fall to the ground. The careful observer will note that both my hands have been drawn up as high as my ears preparatory to the beating of the mat with the hands at the moment of impact.

Unfortunately at this point the cinematographic film came to an end, so that I am not shown actually in contact with the ground.

I do not expect that all my pupils will get so far as this, but some of them find no difficulty whatever in performing this fall from a standing position.

CHAPTER IV

THE THROWS

Mrs. Glasse immortalised herself by one piece of advice, which was first to catch your hare before proceeding to jug it. It may not be quite so essential a preliminary to first throw your man before putting a lock on him, but it is certainly almost as advisable. You may be able to put an opponent, who is quite ignorant of Ju-jutsu, out of action without the preliminary throw, but even then there is a chance that he might possibly work you no inconsiderable damage with his foot or fist while you were bringing your lock into operation, while a practised opponent, however great a novice, is to a certain extent on his guard against all your wiles, until you have disturbed his balance. Frequently it is not only the physical balance which is disturbed, the mental equipoise itself is thrown slightly out of gear, which after all is the ultimate cause of defeat between two equally-matched champions. As long as both remain keenly and perfectly alive to every move of the other, so long will it be impossible for either to apply a triumphant lock.

And really I think that it is in this department of "throws" that Ju-jutsu most *apparently* displays its superiority over ordinary wrestling. The Balance and the Breakfalls may be more reasoned and practised; the Locks, Kata, or defensive movements, and Ground Work generally may be more subtle and scientific. But these finer points are apt to be missed by the uninitiated and uninstructed eye of the man in the street. The feature that appeals to him most of all is the apparent ease with which the small Ju-jutsuan is able to pitch the huge masses of flesh, bone, and muscle which are opposed to him.

These throws may appear miraculous to the ordinary observer, but they are but the natural results of quick movement, balance, and leverage. The lever for which Archimedes asked was by no means such an absurd thing to request as it seemed. A little practice at the various throws explained and shown in the following pages will serve to prove how comparatively small is the muscular exertion required to pitch headlong even an eighteen stone man, once your relative positions have been correctly manœuvred.

I may perhaps be pardoned if I mention here that on one occasion when I was giving a display, a sceptic, who somewhat resented my assertion that gigantic strength was of no avail when pitted against the science of Ju-jutsu, sent for the acknowledged strongest man in the British Army and Navy, in order that I might be compelled to eat my words.

It was while we were preparing for the struggle that one of my pupils, who was assisting me, casually suggested that the merits of Ju-jutsu, as a science, would be more fully displayed were one of his friends who was present, another of my pupils who, by the way, had only been practising the game for about five months, to engage and defeat the giant. The friend in question could be by no means described as a powerful man, while his appearance suggested considerably less power than he actually possessed. So that when he stepped forward to face the gigantic 6ft. 4in. mass of brawn and muscle which confronted him, the contrast was almost laughable. The spectators in fact did laugh, and loudly, especially when the strong man was pitched down helpless and forced to give the signal of defeat after a brief and very one-sided struggle.

I have referred especially to this incident, as it clearly proved the merits of Ju-jutsu in a way that no victory of mine could have done, for at least some of the credit for any triumph which I might achieve would be awarded to my skill and experience as a performer, whereas my pupil gained his laurels by the sheer virtue alone of the science which he had studied under my tuition for such a brief period.

It may perhaps add to the interest of this little anecdote if I mention that I was not aware, nor were any of my friends, of the formidable reputation of our military opponent until after the result. He was sprung upon us without warning and had we been aware of his claims to respect, we should certainly have thought twice before allowing a man who was practically an absolute novice to enter the lists against him in such a public display as this was.

THE ANKLE THROW

(*Made with the left foot*)

THE FIRST ANKLE THROW

THE ANKLE THROW

(*Ashi Harai*, lit., to sweep away the leg)

Hold opponent by the collar with one hand and the sleeve with the other, step back with the left foot and, as opponent brings his left foot forward, place the sole of your right foot against the outside of his left ankle, pushing it across to your left; at the same time pull suddenly and sharply to your right rear with your right hand, flexing the elbow.

THE ANKLE THROW

The foregoing short description of the ankle throw and a glance at the accompanying cinematographic illustration should enable the student to obtain a fair idea of how to practise one of the simplest and yet most effective of the many throws in Ju-jutsu.

Before attempting it, however, he will do well to carefully read through the following.

In the first place, the hold on the collar and sleeve with the right and left hands respectively may be reversed, the left

53

grasping the opponent's collar and the right his sleeve without in any way interfering with the effectiveness of the throw and, in the same way, the stroke with the foot may be made with either foot *as opportunity offers*; that is to say, when your opponent is in the act of stepping forward and *just before* his foot reaches the ground, use the foot immediately opposite his against the outside of his ankle.

In other words, if his right foot is coming forward your left *must* be used, but if you wish to attack his left it must be with your right foot.

In making the stroke with the foot, care should be taken that the leg is kept *quite straight* (the knee should not be bent) and the sole of the foot used; the latter point is an important one, as the use of the side of the foot from the big toe to the ankle bone, is likely to prove a painful experience to both.

The pushing aside of your opponent's foot should be done with a quick sweeping motion and *not* by a kick, as it is often erroneously described.

This will be at once recognised from the literal translations of the Japanese name for the throw—*Ashi*, meaning leg, and *harai*, from *harau*, to sweep, dust, or flick away, as one might brush crumbs or flick away a fly.

NOTE.—Many novices are apt to take up an incorrect position for this throw, and it would be as well to note my position in the single picture illustrating it.

With regard to the pull on the sleeve or collar, this should be carefully observed in the cinematograph illustration, where my pupil's well-drawn-back and well-bent elbow *close into the side* is very clearly and correctly shown.

There, too, the "Breakfall" method is plainly seen, my right arm, fully extended, reaching the ground with a strong blow a fraction of a second before my body.

It is only necessary to add that this throw may be made when walking either forwards or backwards, and that a practical knowledge of it is of considerable assistance to the student in many other throws where the principle of pushing in one direction and pulling in another is used to disturb balance.

To avoid being thrown, raise the foot attacked so that your opponent's attacking foot passes under yours. Here an opportunity for a counter occurs, by catching the attacker's foot in a similar manner as he returns his foot to the ground, making the pull on collar or sleeve as first described.

THE KNEE THROW

(*Hisa guruma*, lit., the Knee Wheel)

Hold opponent by collar and sleeve with right and left hands respectively, step back to the right rear (not directly backwards), pulling opponent with left hand, and when his right foot comes forward place the sole of your left foot against the outside of his

55

knee, at the same time pulling sharply and suddenly with your left hand to your left rear, flexing the elbow.

Photo by L. Gixwant et Cie

THE KNEE THROW

THE KNEE THROW

THE KNEE THROW

As in the Ankle throw, the hold on the collar and sleeve may be reversed and the stroke made with the foot on the right or left side, providing of course the other movements are reversed accordingly.

The initial movement, the steps lightly to the side when walking backwards, tends to make your opponent walk in a sideways direction. This is assisted by the tension on his sleeve which is increased to a sudden jerk as soon as the sole of your foot (the leg being kept quite straight) is in its proper position on the outside of his knee joint, when the same sweeping movement inwards is made (to the right in this case) with the left leg.

On no account should the attacking foot be placed against the knee cap, or front of the knee, and great care should be exercised *not* to kick. I feel that I cannot lay too much emphasis on this point, or remind the student too often of the danger there would be in kicking in this particular throw, as under certain circumstances, or in a certain combination of positions which are quite liable to occur, a kick might easily severely damage the knee joint attacked. And this is a *contretemps* which I am sure no one would desire in an ordinary friendly practice bout.

The most favourable opportunities for this throw occur when the victim is walking forward or turning round, but not when he is walking backwards.

In the cinematographic illustration I should like particularly to draw attention to the main points of the throw, which are most perfectly shown. Note the slight side turn of my pupil's body as the sole of my foot reaches his knee; also that my body is erect, and my left leg perfectly straight during the sweeping movement to the right which finally so completely upsets my pupil's equiiibrium.

The straight extension of his left arm and the swiftness of the movement towards the mat are plain indications of the vigour he is putting into the blow which breaks his fall.

In order to escape being thrown the body should be quickly turned to face the direction of the attacker's raised leg, the knee being bent.

Some assistance may also be gained by using the hand which holds the attacker's coat farthest away from his raised leg, to assist the body in making the turn.

THE CROSS HOOK OR HOCK HOOK

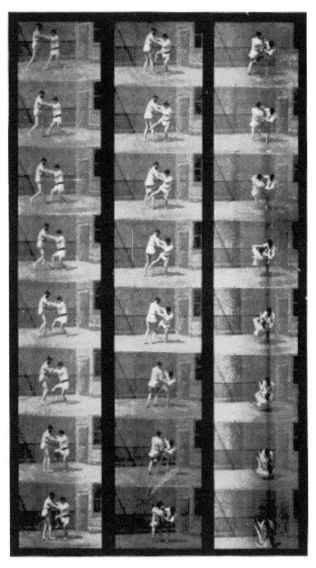

THE CROSS HOOK OR HOCK HOOK THROW

THE CROSS HOOK OR HOCK HOOK

(*Kekaeshi*, from *Kaesu*, to turn over, and *Keru*, to kick.)

The collar and sleeve is held by the right and left hands respectively, and as opponent advances his right foot, engage his right leg at or about the knee joint or hock with your right hock; bend slightly forwards, pull back smartly with your right leg, and at the same time draw him backwards and to your left with your left arm.

THE CROSS HOOK OR HOCK HOOK

The approved method of demonstrating this throw is precisely as illustrated.

The careful observer will note that I have first made a feint at my pupil's left knee, which induces him to step well forward with his right, then with a rapid movement, have hooked him by the hock. In this case the knee is bent, and is swung well back to the rear, so that he may have no chance of slipping out and recovering.

It is necessary to be very careful in attempting this throw, *to be in a strong position*, or in other words, well balanced, for if, in trying to secure the hook, your weight is thrown slightly backwards, it is exceedingly likely that your opponent will have the best of it, and reverse the desired order of things.

Remember, therefore, that your weight should be rather forward, and that it is advantageous to turn the body almost at right angles to its original position, or to the left when using the right leg, as is plainly shown in the cinematographic illustration. This throw may also be made on either side going forwards or backwards, but as it is better to be rather out of the direct line of progress, it will be found easier if the left hand holds your opponent's right sleeve, and your right his collar, when you make the throw with your right, and *vice versa* when you use your left leg.

One may escape being thrown by quickly raising the leg attacked, or by twisting the body so as to face the attacker's back, the latter movement being rather difficult of accomplishment, even to the supple body of one well-trained in Ju-jutsu.

THE HIP THROW

(*Koshi-nage, lit., Hip-throw*)

Hold opponent by lapel and sleeve with right and left hand respectively, and as opponent advances his right foot, pivot sharply on your left heel (which is to the rear) to your left, swinging your hips well under your opponent by bending the knees; then keeping the feet together, pull with your left hand, bend forward and straighten the knees.

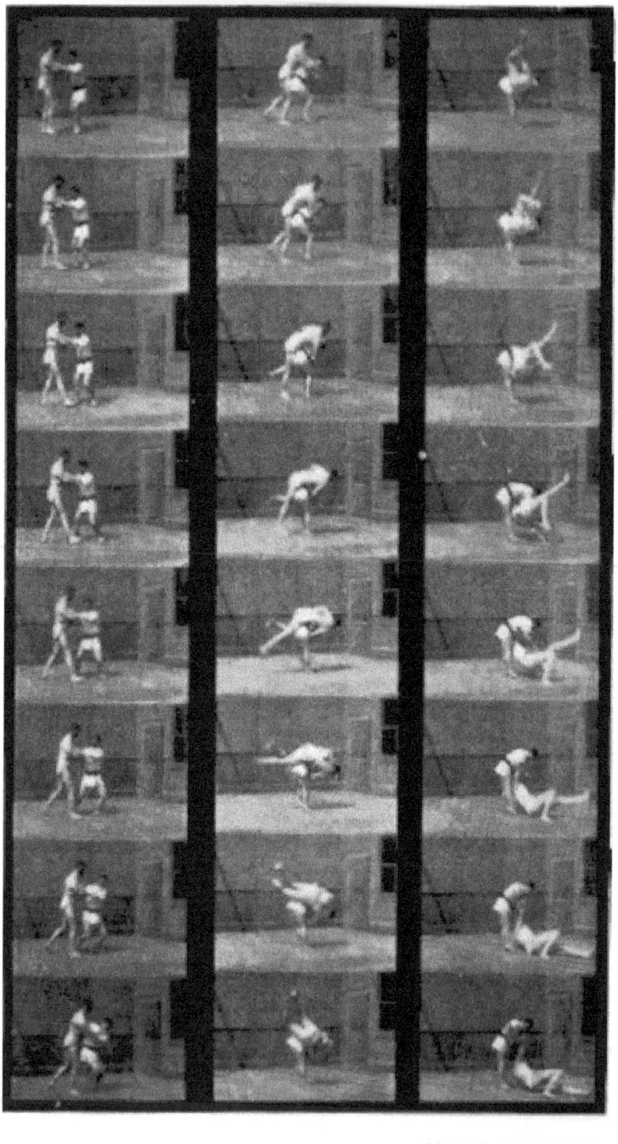

Photo by L. Gaumont et Cie

THE HIP THROW

THE HIP THROW

THE HIP THROW

In this throw, the position of the hands may be reversed and it may of course be made either to the left or to the right.

The pull with the left hand, if the throw is being made as in the illustration, is most important and should not be forgotten, as it is rather apt to be in such a combination of movements as that just described.

The success of the throw depends mainly on the rapidity with which the body is turned and assumes the correct position.

The walking and balance practice previously described, wherein so much importance is attached to the avoidance of muscular tension at all times, to the looseness of the hips and general freedom of movement, will materially assist the serious student to assume this position, the finish of the throw being a comparatively easy matter.

I find, when watching my pupils, that a very frequent cause of failure at the critical moment of the throw, i.e., just as the turn of the body has been made, is due to the fact that they forgot to bend the knees when getting under their opponent's, the result being that they have no *lifting power*.

But if the knees are bent when the turn of the body has been made, and the hip is close into and well under one's opponent, the straightening of the knees (a relatively very slight muscular effort) causes him to lose his grip of the ground, or foothold, while the tilt of the body, assisted by the pull on his lapel or sleeve as the case may be, brings him to the ground with a very slight expenditure of muscular energy.

In this, as in practically every other throw, success is mainly dependent on *quickness*, and in the same way the guard must be made almost intuitively if the attack is made, as it should be, with great rapidity.

If the throw is being made as in the illustration it is only necessary to place the left hand against the attacker's hip as his body is turning in, and thus prevent him getting under you.

In this, as almost throughout the practice of Ju-jutsu, the quicker wins.

THE SPRING HIP THROW

THE SPRING HIP THROW

THE SPRING HIP THROW

(*Hanegoshi*, Spring-hip)

Hold opponent by collar and sleeve and, when walking backwards, draw him slightly towards you as you step back with your left foot; raise your right leg till your shin crosses his thighs, then as you bend to the left (at the hips) pull firmly with your left hand.

THE SPRING HIP THROW

This throw is in some particulars somewhat similar to the Hip throw, but in my opinion is a rather better example of true leverage, for whereas in the latter throw (the "Hip") when you draw your opponent's body across your hips you straighten your slightly bent knees and so lift him off the ground, in this he is fairly levered from his feet at the start.

In the cinematographic illustration it will be noted that my pupil has slightly bent his left leg, but this is not necessary and was, doubtless, mainly due to the fact that he is considerably taller than I am.

It is also evident by the position of my body while falling, that he has got rather more impetus into the throw than would be usual, and certainly more than is necessary, but of course it is none the less effective for that.

The most important thing to remember is that, at the moment of turning your body, as your left foot steps back and to the left, your opponent's body should be CLOSE to yours, otherwise the lever movement will be quite impossible. And here the similarity between the two throws is perhaps more noticeable by the fact that the same guard applies to both. The bodies must be close together to obtain the necessary lift or leverage. The defence is to keep the bodies apart, in order that this may not be effected, and, by simply placing your hand against your opponent's hip and staving yourself off, so to speak, at the critical moment, you are rendered safe for the time being—if you have been *quick enough* to anticipate his move.

THE PULL OVER OR SIDE THROW

(*Hiki-otoshi*, to pull-drop)

Hold opponent in the usual manner by collar and sleeve and, as you step back with the left, turn your body slightly to the left and quickly bring your right leg across, placing your right foot in such a manner that it reaches the ground just beyond and immediately in front of your opponent's approaching right. Pull quickly and strongly with your left hand across your outstretched right leg.

71

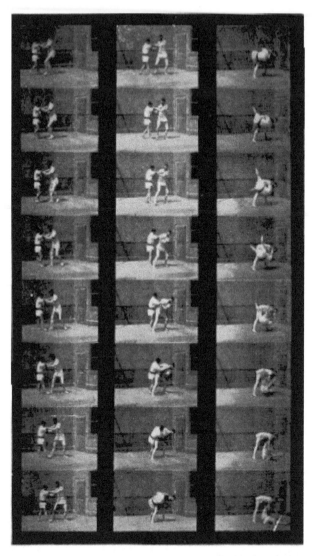

Photo by L. Gaumont et Cie

THE PULL OVER OR SIDE THROW

THE PULL OVER OR SIDE THROW

(From a kneeling position)

73

THE PULL OVER OR SIDE THROW

The quick turn of the body and the crossing over of the right leg to its position in front of your opponent's must be well timed and rapidly executed. If too soon, he will have no difficulty in stepping over your outstretched leg, and if too late, his left foot will already be advancing to assist him in maintaining his balance, or resisting the throw.

As your right foot takes up its position, pull sharply and strongly with your left hand, paying particular attention to the direction of the pull.

This should be immediately across your own body with your elbow bent to the left side, and not in the direction your opponent is going. It is this side pull that so completely disturbs his balance, making him fall sideways on to his back over your obstructing leg. This is most admirably and clearly shown in the illustration.

One might ask, "What difference does it make whether you throw your man sideways or straight forward?" and the answer is simple enough.

Although you timed the throw correctly, the chances are, as forward progression is the most natural to man, he will far more likely be able to save himself, and therefore a clean fall would seldom result, but side movement being most awkward for him, he has little or no chance of recovery.

As will be seen in the cinematographic illustration, my

pupil has pulled me rather close in to him and consequently I was pulled over his leg, rather higher up than was usual. The approved position, however, is very clearly shown in the single pose photographs where I am making the throw.

The two photographs show the throw in operation from both a standing and a kneeling position.

THE PULL OVER OR SIDE THROW

(From a standing position)

THE SHOULDER THROW

THE SHOULDER THROW

(*Se-o-i-nage*, shoulder-throw)

Hold opponent in the usual manner by collar and sleeve.

When walking backwards step back with the left foot, pivoting quickly to the left till you are facing the same direction as your opponent, and bending both knees with the feet not too far apart. Get well under and directly in front of him, straighten your legs and bend forward and downwards, assisting with a pull mainly from the left hand, so that your opponent is drawn on to your back and thrown directly over your right shoulder.

THE SHOULDER THROW

If the illustrations are carefully followed, the student will have no difficulty in seeing exactly how this body-twist is made. He will be able to place himself in the necessary positions, first slowly and afterwards more rapidly, till what at first appeared an awkward turn to execute, becomes a simple movement. While the left leg is drawn back, the body is turning slightly to the left, so that when the foot reaches the ground it is able to support the body during the pivot and until the right leg has had time to follow round to its position beside the left.

It then assists in carrying the weight of your opponent's body, which, by the time the turn is complete, should already be in close contact with your own and ready for the tilting or lever motion, applied by the straightening of your legs and the consequent raising of your back.

As the legs are straightened, your body is bent forward and downward, and the pull on your opponent's coat is increased till the rotary movement, caused by the raising of his feet from the ground and the downward approach of his head, is completed and he is thrown directly over your right shoulder on to his back.

THE SHOULDER THROW

It is of the utmost importance that the twist of the body should be made rapidly, and, though the student may find some little difficulty at first in getting into the correct position with bent legs while in the act of walking backwards, constant practice will work wonders, and in a comparatively short time he should be able to make the turn sufficiently rapidly to enable him to throw an opponent with little or practically no exertion to himself.

SECOND ANKLE THROW

(*O Kuri-ashi*, from *O Kuru*, send away or carry away, *ashi*, legs)

Hold opponent in the usual manner, and when he walks sideways, not by crossing his legs but by bringing one foot up to the other to the left, place the sole of your left foot outside his right ankle, when his feet are apart.

Then, at the moment when he starts to bring his right foot up to his left, sweep his foot swiftly to your right and lift him up with your hands.

THE SECOND ANKLE THROW

THE SECOND ANKLE THROW

SECOND ANKLE THROW

In the chapter on balance I have already mentioned the difficulty that human beings experience in walking sideways, and we now come to a throw designed to be used only when moving in a sideways direction. This particular movement may be seen when the military command, "Dress" or "Dress up," is given, it being necessary for men standing shoulder to shoulder to close up, or to get into line, if too far apart.

It consists of a step to the left (if moving to the left) with the left foot, the right being brought up to it.

Now in the practice of Ju-jutsu, when it becomes necessary to move sideways, this step is often made at varying speeds, sometimes slowly and sometimes quickly.

If your opponent makes this step and you desire to utilise this throw, you must time your leg stroke at his ankle just at the moment he is bringing one leg up to the other, as in the illustration, and instead of allowing it to be placed solidly on the ground next to the other, continue the stroke and sweep him off his legs. In order to accomplish this, however, it is necessary to use your hands.

These movements should take as much of the weight off his feet as possible and so render the sweeping movement very much easier.

It may seem almost incredible that a man can be apparently

lifted clean off his feet in this manner, but the reason is simple enough. The throw is made in the direction of progression and his legs are forced in the direction of their movement, his body being lifted at the moment that he jumps.

It is, therefore, the combination of assisted movements which produces such unexpected results.

The student must give particular attention to the timing of the leg stroke, for if this is incorrectly judged, the stroke itself will be of no avail, and no amount of the lifting movement will compensate the error.

The cinema photographs of this throw clearly show the "Break-fall" method in application, my arm being very plainly seen on the ground after the blow, *before* my body arrives there.

THIRD ANKLE THROW

OR

ANKLE ROLL

(*Yoko-Sutemi*, side-give-oneself-up or sacrifice oneself)

Hold opponent by collar and sleeve in the usual manner, then, when walking backwards, take a step to the right with the right foot and sit down quickly, close to the heel of your right foot.

While in the act of sitting place the sole of your left against opponent's right ankle as it comes forward, and pull smartly with your left hand on opponent's sleeve.

ANKLE ROLL

As I have already stated that many of the tricks and throws in Ju-jutsu are dangerous, I would again like to remind students, particularly those who are unable to secure the assistance of an expert to coach them in their preliminary attempts, that it is advisable to use the utmost care when practising with a friend, even at the risk of being considered a little over-cautious.

I should like to repeat, in order that the pupil may avoid unnecessary risks, that such throws as the one I am now describing should be done very slowly and deliberately for the first few times, or a damaged shoulder or collar-bone may very easily result.

At the same time I may say that if the "Ha-uchi" or method of "Breaking Fall" has been well learned, there need be little fear of hurting oneself.

In the preliminary description of this throw I have again started with the usual hold. This, as in most other throws, may be reversed and the throw made in equally good style. In the ordinary practice or contest it should be made on either side as may be expedient, or as the chance occurs.

THE THIRD ANKLE THROW OR ANKLE ROLL

Plate by L. Gaumont et Cie

THE THIRD ANKLE THROW OR ANKLE ROLL

88

When the side step, which enables one to assume the sitting position, is made, just clear of the opponent's line of progression, the pull on opponent's sleeve or collar, as the case may be, begins; this naturally induces him to bring forward the leg that is to the rear.

In the ordinary way he would do this as he is walking forward, but if by any chance he should hesitate, the pull will help him to make up his mind, as it were, and will prevent the sudden halt which would be fatal to the throw at this juncture.

And now, if the timing of the side step has been correct—as in the illustration—there should be no difficulty in catching your opponent's right leg at the ankle with the sole of your left foot. The force of the fall will be governed, first by the attraction of gravity, secondly by tension or the amount of pull on his sleeve, and thirdly in ratio to the rate of his progression at the time it was made. The word *utemi* conveys the exact meaning of this throw, since it may be literally translated "to sacrifice oneself," or "to throw oneself away," to which I may add in this case, "in order to gain an advantage." It is a most useful throw and one which plainly demonstrates the simple strategy on which the whole fabric of Ju-jutsu is built up.

STOMACH THROW

(*Sutemi*, give oneself up or sacrifice oneself)

Hold opponent in the usual manner and, when walking backwards or when opponent is stooping forward, quickly raise your foot, with the leg well to the middle of his stomach.

At the same time sit down quickly and continue the movement of your opponent's body by straightening your leg as soon as you feel his weight well balanced on it.

THE STOMACH THROW

THE STOMACH THROW

THE STOMACH THROW

This is another throw that should be practised very carefully and, as a further warning, I feel it my duty to repeat that too much care cannot be exercised till the trick or throw is *thoroughly* mastered.

It is one of the most effective and most showy throws in Ju-jutsu, and is comparatively easy to learn.

If, when practising, your opponent assumes the attitude so generally noticed in various other forms of wrestling—leaning forward at an angle that is dangerous as far as his body balance is concerned—you should have no difficulty in seizing the opportunity. Slip quickly on to your back, at the same time raise your foot to his middle—*getting wel under him*. Pull on his sleeve and collar and straighten your leg when he is fairly balanced, but not till then, when he will be sent flying over your head clear on to his back and, unless these movements are done very carefully, or your opponent is well versed in "Breaking Fall," he will probably come down with such a bump as to shake him up very thoroughly. By all means, therefore, let your opponent down lightly by giving him some measure of support with your hands as he turns in the air, so that he may treat you likewise when it comes to your own turn.

The main safeguard against this throw is to keep erect at all times when practising, and if an attempt should be made on you by your opponent, a quick body turn or swing with the

93

hips will cause his foot to slip harmlessly to one side, whereby he will miss the fulcrum that would otherwise enable him to lever you over his head.

It is in such movements as these that the practical utility of the loose hips comes in, for the man with a stiffened body would find it extremely difficult to make the necessary twist with sufficient speed to avert a clever and sudden attack.

In the photographs illustrating this throw my pupil may be plainly observed breaking his fall with both hands and feet, but where possible I would suggest that the method referred to in the chapter on "Ha-uchi" or "Breaking-Fall," should be adopted.

I refer to the third method, which consists of a forward roll and hip twist before the turn is complete, so that if the twist is made to the left, the left arm and the outside of the left leg and the sole of the right foot, which is brought in front of the left by crossing the legs, beat the mat simultaneously.

THE SCISSORS

THE SCISSORS

THE SCISSORS

(*Kugi-nuki*, lit., pincers)

Hold opponent by sleeve with left hand (the other hand need not hold necessarily) and, as opponent walks backward, swing the left leg in front of his thighs and the right behind his hocks, with the right hand resting on the ground. Retain hold with left hand on his sleeve, press backwards with your left leg, keeping the right leg rigid, pressing forwards against his hocks.

THE SCISSORS

To attain the position necessary to effect this throw may appear very difficult at first, but by practising it several times quite slowly, it will soon be found a simple matter to jump into position. The timing of the chance requires careful noting, as it is very important.

By this I mean that the jump to position should be made, as is very clearly shown in the illustration, just as your opponent's weight is evenly supported on both his legs, the one nearest to your attack being forward (*i.e.*, his right).

The same opportunity may be taken when he is walking either backwards or forwards, and may be made from directly in front or rather more easily when you are nearer to one side (the one about to be attacked).

The reason for the fall is a very simple one and will doubtless have already been noticed by the reader.

When you first deliver your attack your opponent's body is moving backwards and his balance is in the act of being transferred to his left foot. By the time you reach him, his forward (right) leg is about to be moved back to catch his balance, but it is prevented from doing this by your retaining right leg, so that with however slight an additional impulse the impact of your body has given him, the scissor-like pressure of your legs completes the disturbance of his balance in the original direction in which he was moving.

If he is coming forward, the only point of difference is that you disturb his balance in the direction opposite to which he is progressing, but this does not interfere with the effectiveness of the throw, though it may possibly appear to the beginner to be slightly more difficult than when he is moving backwards.

CHAPTER V

LOCKS

The following are a few of the many locks or holds by which the exponent of Ju-jutsu is able to reduce an opponent to submission.

They may be said to consist mainly of the application of leverage where an opponent is at an anatomical disadvantage.

The leverage is applied in such a manner that the portion of the anatomy attacked is liable to disablement. It is at this moment, in a friendly contest, when the victim, feeling the pressure becoming more than he can comfortably bear, and at the same time one from which he cannot relieve himself, gives the signal of defeat. This should consist of one or two distinct taps or beats on the ground or your own or opponent's body, with your hand or foot or both, as may be easiest.

I think it important to impress on all my readers that this signal should be as distinct as possible so that there can be no possible chance of its not being instantly recognised, for failure in this may result in a regrettable accident. Indeed, I have known of one case in which arms have been accidentally damaged for the simple reason that the wretched victim had actually forgotten what to do when defeated. This may sound incredible, and I should scarcely believe it myself had I not heard it from the victim's own lips.

For the same reason, the student who applies the lock should be most careful in putting on the pressure, as he is quite certain not to realise at first what a very slight strain is sufficient, if the positions are absolutely correct.

On no account should it be applied with a jerk, or damage to your opponent may easily result, and I may add that it is my earnest hope that none of those who take up the study of this fascinating game may have the misfortune to be the victims of carelessness, or suffer through the negligence of others in this direction. It is, I trust, needless to add that failure to grant immediate release to the victim would be unsportsmanlike to the last degree, as at this point of the game trifling of any sort is quite inadmissible.

It is quite probable that the tyro will find it difficult to manœuvre so as to secure some of these holds, but he will learn much by trying to obtain them in a friendly bout, remembering always that quickness of movement and change of tactics are important factors to success.

I may say that I hope at some future time to be able to write an advanced treatise devoted particularly to "groundwork," in which I shall endeavour to make clear the (sometimes) rather complicated movements that are most useful and necessary during a struggle on the ground.

THE ARM LOCK

(*Ude nata*, arm break)

Perhaps one of the best known locks in this country is that known as the arm lock, owing to the fact that it has been used so generally in contest work on the stage here.

It has the merit of being quite clear to the onlookers that an arm has been trapped and at the same time, owing to the relative positions of the contestants when the signal of defeat is given, the spectators are able to see it, there being very little chance of the victor's body obstructing the view, as is sometimes the case with other locks.

The first chance for applying it occurs just after you have thrown your man by, say, the ankle throw, when you retain hold of your opponent's sleeve, keeping his body a little off the ground on the near side.

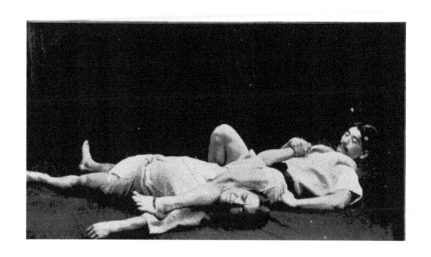

THE ARM LOCK

THE SECOND ARM LOCK

That is to say—we will suppose that I have thrown my assistant with my left foot against his right ankle—I have retained my hold of his right sleeve (having released my hold afterwards on the completion of the position, when there was no further occasion for retaining it), and caught his right wrist, my thumb crossing his, with my right hand and thrown my left leg across his neck, while my right leg is tucked close up under his armpit in the manner shown, or may be, across his chest (a very excellent and strong position). The position itself is fairly simple. And now for the important points.

I hold the victim's arm securely nipped by my thighs with my left leg across his neck, then, keeping his thumb up, I press his right hand slowly down towards my chest and, if necessary, slightly raise my hips from the ground to increase the pressure, at the same time straightening my left leg as far as may be necessary.

The strain is on the victim's elbow joint, and a very trifling amount of it is quite sufficient to compel submission.

Great care should be taken when getting into the position not to handle his arm roughly. By that I mean *don't* start by gripping it tightly into your chest and keeping it thus throughout the movement till you are on your back, or you may damage it before you are aware, but you may, and in fact you should, get your legs into position as rapidly as possible so as to secure a good hold with them above his elbow joint, when the leverage on the arm may be applied at your leisure.

It is just as well, perhaps, again to sound a warning note to the man in the lock who may be inclined to think that he can escape easily.

If the position is once assumed and the pressure on the arm attacked already started, extreme care should be used if any struggling to escape is attempted, as it is more than likely that in making it the victim will damage his own arm.

At this point it is *too late* to struggle, and the contestant will be well advised if he gracefully gives in and, profiting by the experience gained, uses it in future practice when opportunity offers.

To further demonstrate how the arm lock is applied during a struggle on the ground, I show here a very usual method, the opportunity for which obtains almost invariably, if your opponent has not studied Ju-jutsu.

It will be seen that I am astride my pupil's body, a very strong and useful position, and one to be striven for during a struggle on this account.

It will be readily understood that the under man will naturally do something to protect himself, or to try and throw his assailant off, and to do so will probably try to push him away with outstretched arm, or he may try to catch him by the collar (as here shown).

Now is the time to act; my pupil's right hand is on my collar, so I bring up my right foot to assist the swing of my body to my left as I catch his arm securely with both my hands. Then I bring my left leg rapidly round, till it clips his arm and comes down across his neck, when I roll over to the final position on my back, and put on the pressure till I hear or feel the signal.

THE SECOND ARM LOCK

This arm lock as shown in the photograph is about as complete a "tie-up" as one could wish to have. My pupil is in a particularly helpless position, and anyone caught in a similar hold soon realises that an attempt to struggle would only be liable to result in injury to himself.

To secure it I first assumed a sitting posture beside my pupil, with my left arm round his neck and my left leg under his left arm close into his body, my right leg being extended simply to assist, if necessary, in maintaining my equilibrium.

In trying to get away, the left arm of the victim is brought into play, probably at my neck, collar, or sleeve, or even against my legs, so that it is possible at almost any moment for me to catch his left wrist with my right hand and press his extended arm down and across my left thigh, the palm of his hand being kept up. As soon as it reaches this point it is quite an easy matter to get my left heel over his wrist; and to make the hold quite secure, my right leg is drawn up, as shown in the photograph, in such a manner as to prevent his arm slipping beyond my retaining heel, or my heel from slipping beyond his hand.

To cause submission I only have to raise my left hip slightly, when the tension at his elbow joint becomes such that the signal is soon given.

A careful study of the photograph should enable anyone to get the position quite correctly, and, once having done so, there should be no difficulty in repeating it in a friendly contest.

Care should be taken when pressing the victim's arm down across the thigh and when getting the heel over his wrist, as, once his arm is extended, it requires very slight pressure indeed to do serious damage.

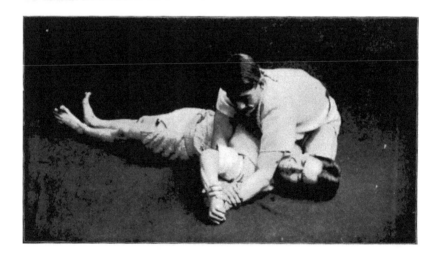

THIRD ARM LOCK

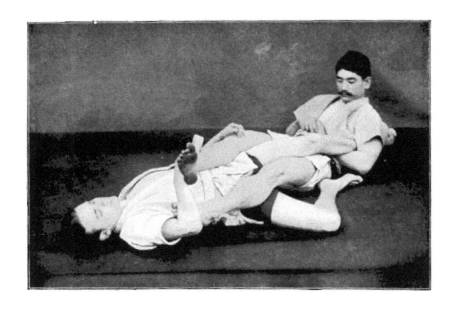

THE LEG LOCK

THE THIRD ARM LOCK

Having shown arm locks from the prone and sitting positions, I now give one that may be applied when kneeling.

Suppose that you have been trying unsuccessfully to secure the second arm lock and that your opponent's struggles assist you to your knees, you will probably find, if you are still trying to hold him down, that your body is leaning across his. You should then catch his left wrist with your left hand (so that your little finger is nearest to his hand) and press it down towards the ground; next bring your right hand, as I have brought mine in the photograph, under your opponent's upper arm, so that you can catch your own left wrist with your right hand. Having once secured the grip, start levering up with your right arm so as to bring your opponent's elbow in a forward and upward direction.

If he happens to be very supple in the joints, it may be necessary to continue the leverage until his elbow is brought almost up to his ear before he feels any discomfort, but in the ordinary way most people cannot stand very much of it before their shoulders begin to warn them that the strain is getting dangerous, and they are only too glad to be relieved by giving the signal in the usual way.

THE LEG LOCK

(*Ashi nata*, leg break)

The leg hold, or lock, shown in this illustration, may be applied in a standing as well as in a prone position, and in several different ways as regards the relative positions of the combatants; but in effect they are precisely similar, the vulnerable point being the same.

In this case it is not a joint that is attacked, but the lower point of the calf muscle.

The following is the method of procedure. I have first had

hold of my pupil's left ankle, while I was standing up, he being on his back; then I have tucked it well up under my left arm, so that his instep is against my armpit, my left forearm, with the sharp edge of the bone upwards, against the lower extremity of his calf. Now I assume a sitting posture, throwing my left leg inside his left leg and over his right before actually reaching the ground, and gripping his left thigh between mine, thus holding him securely.

Then my right leg is rapidly extended on the outside of his left leg and across his body, to assist in maintaining his leg in a suitable position for the pressure.

This is applied as I straighten my legs (which prevent him from rising) by bending my body back and so raising my left forearm against the lower point of his calf, as already indicated.

My right hand grasps my left hand and keeps my left forearm rigid, while the pressure gradually increases as my body bends backwards till the signal is given.

Opportunities for this hold frequently occur in practice, as the student will find from experience, and it may be applied practically in direct sequence to the Scissors throw.

THE NECK HOLD, OR LOCK

FIRST POSITION

This hold or lock is perhaps one of the most popular in the whole range comprising this section of Ju-jutsu practice, and I should think runs the Arm lock very close for first place.

The main reason for this is no doubt on account of its complete effectiveness.

It may be said to somewhat resemble the knock-out blow in English boxing, in that a man may be very easily rendered unconscious, but, in my opinion, it is infinitely more humane and, I might say, almost artistic.

Humane, because there is no possible chance of a broken jaw or ribs, or indeed any material damage of that kind. Artistic, because the victim suffers nothing, or at the most very trifling discomfort, before (if he so chooses, by purposely refraining to give the signal that he appreciates his inability to proceed) being wafted off to the land of dreams. There is no smashing blow and a victim involuntarily unconscious; there is always time—ample time—not only for the full recognition of the seriousness of the position, but also to signify one's knowledge and appreciation of that fact by giving the usual signal.

What more complete finale to either a friendly contest or a serious bout could there be than this?

THE NECK HOLD OR LOCK

(First Position)

THE NECK HOLD OR "LOCK" FROM UNDERNEATH

(Second Position)

For my part, in stage contest work I only use it occasionally as a change, but feeling sometimes that my audience are not quite educated up to it, I generally use the Arm lock, which strikes me always as being particularly clear and most easily understood by those who have but a very trifling, or even no, knowledge of the game at all.

Before proceeding to describe the hold I should like to disabuse the minds of those who may imagine, perhaps very naturally, that it is a "strangle" hold, as it is so often and, like a good many other points connected with Ju-jutsu, so erroneously called.

It is in no sense a "strangle" (though it may be made so), as the victim's windpipe is not necessarily interfered with, and I think this will be readily understood by all who will carefully read through the method of procedure.

In the first place it will be noted from the illustration that I am above my assistant, kneeling on my right knee (practically squatting on my right heel) on the left side of his body my left leg is thrown over his body and my left foot on the ground close in to the ribs.

With my right hand I have caught his collar well round to the right side of his neck, my left having been slipped under my right arm to a similar position on the left side of his neck. I am now in a position to begin the pressure. This is done by giving the wrists a twist so that the palms of the hands are turned in an upward direction, while the bones of the hand from the first finger knuckle to the wrist (if the hold has been caught deep enough) press against either side of the victim's neck at a point below the ears. The arms are then bent and, by a cross pull as our bodies draw closer together, the pressure is increased. In what may be called the upper position (here described) I have the weight of my body to assist my arms in their scissors-like action on the throat, should it happen to be necessary.

In regard to the position I have taken at the start, I should like to mention that it is a very strong one, for it is favourable if you wish to retain the upper position, balance being comparatively easily adjusted during the victim's struggles. The loss of the upper position is, however, not necessarily fatal to the finish of the hold, as it may be, and frequently is, used from the underneath. (See following illustration.)

Another position often taken for this hold is when you are astride or kneeling across your opponent, this may be easily changed to that already described, or *vice versa*.

If your opponent is able to roll you over from this position when both your hands are holding his collar, keep your knees close in to his sides and lock them round his waist, retaining in this manner your relative positions without losing your grip on his collar and steadily increasing the pressure. If the correct hold has been taken in the first instance and carefully maintained, it is difficult for even an expert to escape.

THE NECK HOLD OR LOCK (FROM UNDERNEATH)

SECOND POSITION

In Ju-jutsu, contrary to the styles of wrestling in vogue in this and other European countries, in which a combatant is practically vanquished as soon as he is on his back, this may often be a very strong position, from which it is easily possible to "finish" an adversary by one of the locks applicable to such a case.

The Neck lock is one of these, and the most favourable position is most plainly shown in the photograph.

In the first place, my legs are round my assistant's waist, my right hand is holding his left sleeve and my left hand his jacket collar on his left side.

The position of my left hand is important.

I get it well round almost to the back of his neck at the start, then, with as rapid a movement as possible, I bring my right hand under my left arm (slipping it under will generally be found much easier than over), and catch his collar on the right side of his neck as far behind as I can. When my hold is once secured I bring my feet on to his thighs and, as I straighten my legs slightly to prevent him from rising to his feet, I pull him down towards me, twisting my wrists just sufficiently to bring the upper edge or bone of my forearms against the sides of his neck, exerting the while a scissor-like action with my arms as the space between my elbows increases and his chest gets nearer to mine.

If the pressure has been properly applied at the right spot—this should be at a point in the neck just below the ear—and with the hard bone of the wrist just at the base of the thumb, the victim, though not suffering pain to any extent, may be rendered helpless or even unconscious in precisely the same manner as previously described.

His endeavours to escape are generally in the direction of getting on to his feet, or over the retaining legs that are either against his thighs, as in the illustration, or round his waist. These attempts must be frustrated, for if he is once free from the grip of your legs he is able to render the hold on his neck quite ineffective by swinging his body round towards that arm of his opponent which is undermost below his chin, unwinding himself, so to speak, from the grip. In the case of the illustration this would be to my right, or my assistant's left side.

THIRD NECK HOLD "C"

THE SECOND NECK HOLD

THE SECOND NECK HOLD

It is often the case during a contest after a throw, or perhaps an attempt at one, that the contestants become separated, when the one regaining his feet or recovering his lost balance, as the case may be, must always be most careful how he does so, and it is to show the student how particularly necessary it is *not* to get up with the head bent down or looking at the ground, but keeping an ever watchful eye on his opponent, that I now show the manner in which he would most likely be caught, should he fail to bear this little bit of advice in mind.

The photograph shows the relative positions very much better than any words of mine could describe them, and it is only necessary to give some little explanation of the actual hold, to enable anyone to test its effectiveness for himself.

I have caught my pupil round the neck with my right arm, just as he helped himself from his knees on to his feet, in what I should think would be the most ordinary manner (from "all fours"), namely, first bringing one foot up to the ground, then pushing up with the hands and getting on to the other foot, or bringing it up to the assistance of the first. During this movement the body has been bent forward the whole time, and it was just before he straightened his body that I caught him with my right arm.

My forearm is brought close up under his chin so that the upper edge or sharp bone of the forearm is under his throat.

118

My left hand catches my right, which is now closed (with the thumb uppermost) and, by pressing upwards, assists it in retaining the hold.

When it is necessary to increase the pressure, the back is slightly hollowed and the shoulders gradually thrown back precisely as shown in the photograph, where I have just started the strain.

If in his struggles to free himself the victim brings you to the ground, you should make sure of wrapping your legs round his body at his waist, when your position is even stronger than before.

The body held with your legs will prevent him from moving in the direction of the strain which, in relation to your body, is upwards, and it must be a strong neck indeed that can stand much of this.

THE THIRD NECK HOLD (FROM BEHIND)

(a)

Having given an illustration of what may occur if an eye is not kept on an opponent, I have thought it advisable to show the danger of turning one's back during a contest either when standing or struggling on the ground.

In the first photograph I show the hold in its simplest form, and the student who has studied the previous one will at once

119

see that it is practically the same in effect, though the positions differ somewhat.

It will be well if he bears this in mind, as it will help him to remember a little point that he might otherwise forget.

It will be seen that my right arm encircles my pupil's neck and, though from a different position to the one previously described, the adjustment of the forearm is precisely the same, the upper edge or bone of the forearm pressing close in to the throat.

In the same manner, my left hand supports my right assisting to maintain the position.

The tighter I draw in my forearm across my pupil's throat, the more discomfort he feels, but to give full effect to the hold, it is necessary to press my shoulder forward against the back of his head.

This latter movement is of great importance and resembles the throwing back of my shoulders in the last hold, when the pressure on the back of the head is developed at the lower end of the back of my shoulder or armpit.

In the case of a very strong opponent who might catch my arm strongly in the manner shown by my pupil in the photograph, the pressure on the neck might be somewhat diminished, but this would not prevent the full effect of the pressure from my shoulder.

The angle of my pupil's body to the ground is particularly suitable; if he were more upright the difficulty of pressing against the back of his head with my shoulder would be increased, and I should probably change my hold to his collar with either my left or right hand, whichever was most convenient (as shown in the illustration B).

THIRD NECK HOLD "A"

THIRD NECK HOLD "B"

(*b*)

In this photograph I have his right arm secured by my right arm and right knee, while the grip with my left hand on his coat collar on the right side of his neck enables me to press my shoulder forward against the back of his head, and, by the drawing back of my elbow, which helps my shoulder pressure, I increase the strain on his neck.

At the least tension now the hand that has caught my arm is quickly released and a couple of taps on my forearm immediately apprise me of the fact that—it is enough.

(*c*)

Another picture (facing page 94) shows a combination hold which includes the neck hold just described.

Here I have my pupil by this neck hold with my left arm and, squatting on my left heel, I have brought my right foot forward, so that my knee is about on a level with his shoulder.

I have caught his right wrist and drawn his right arm across my shin. I have now only to increase the strain by pressing forward with my knee, or by bracing the knee and pulling back with my right hand, to make him realise that his arm is in danger.

If I add to this the forward pressure of my left shoulder, and the pull back against his throat with my left hand, the signal is given in a hurry, when immediate release promptly follows and no damage is done.

CHAPTER VI

A WORD PORTRAIT

BY

PERCY LONGHURST

It is possible that the reader will be interested in learning somewhat relating personally to the talented author of this volume, itself perhaps the most valuable treatise on the Japanese art of *Ju-jutsu*—otherwise *Judo*—that has been published, so simply and lucidly stated are the movements required for the correct performance of the holds, throws, locks, etc., dealt with; so lacking is it in those elements of the sensational which some writers upon the subject of the "soft art" have thought proper to embellish their compilations. It is further possible that readers will find interest in becoming acquainted with the development of Ju-jutsu outside Japan since its introduction into England by Mr. Uyenishi and his compatriot, Yukio Tani, nearly forty years ago.

I knew Sada Kazu Uyenishi (stage name "Raku"). No

particular merit attaches thereto, but I was among the first of the English wrestlers and athletes upon whom he demonstrated the wonderful efficiency of the art which some, even to-day, still persist in referring to as "Japanese wrestling." The Japanese themselves term it a "war exercise," the art of self defence. They are utilitarians, and when Ju-jutsu was developed they had no conception of it as a sport, an athletic recreation. It was—and to them is—a serious exercise for a serious purpose.

Uyenishi was a pastmaster of the art and a brilliant teacher. It was his teaching, the lessons I had from him, that gave me the convincing proof of the genuine value of Ju-jutsu as the best means yet devised to accomplish the purpose for which it was intended. Uyenishi's talent as an instructor was equal to his skill as an exponent. In his many music hall contests (which he abandoned to become a teacher) there was none of the theatrical element, the playing to the gallery, the attempt to "make a fool" of his opponent. I imagine it never entered his mind that he was providing the spectators with an entertainment.

A sportsman according to the best Western standards, a gentleman, an artist in his own way, this be-spectacled young Japanese, whose refined appearance carried no suggestion of his astonishing physical qualities and powers, a muscular development of all-over excellence that was a delight to the eye, made friends wherever he went.

Expert swimmer—he dived fully clothed from Queen's

Bridge, Belfast, to effect the rescue and restoration (by methods known only to expert practisers of *Ju-jutsu*) of a drowning man. Competent in the arts of *Roku-shaku-bo* and *Han-bo*, exercises nearly resembling the old English quarterstaff and singlestick play, he was a front rank exponent of *Kenjutsu*, the "sword-art" of Japan. Sada Kazu Uyenishi was one never to be forgotten, however brief the acquaintance.

PROFESSOR S. K. UYENISHI

S. K. UYENISHI AT HOME IN OSAKA

I have written "was", because, having relinquished his teaching school in London, and his position as instructor in *Ju-jutsu* at the Headquarters Army Gymnasium at Aldershot, Uyenishi decided to return to his own country, where his death took place a number of years ago.

For the benefit of those interested in the more personal details concerning Uyenishi, it may be mentioned that he was born at Osaka in 1880; he was thus rather more than twenty years of age when he, with Yukio Tani, was brought to England

128

by Mr. Barton-Wright, an English engineer long resident in Japan and a pupil of the Japanese *dojos* (schools of *Ju-jutsu* instruction). It will be agreed that his physical development was unusually good.

	Normal	Expanded or flexed
Height	5 feet, 5 inches	
Weight ..	9 st. 2 lb.	
Neck	15 in. ..	16½ in.
Chest	34 in. ..	37¼ in.
Waist	28 in.	
Thigh	20 in. ..	21¼ in.
Calf	14 in. ..	14½ in.
Biceps	12¼ in. ..	14 in.
Forearm ..	10¾ in. ..	11½ in.
Wrist	7 in.	

The student of physical culture will not fail to note the unusual extent of Uyenishi's powers of neck expansion. I was present at a display he gave, part of which served to demonstrate the extraordinary strength his neck muscles possessed.

One of the feats was to escape from beneath a stout bamboo pole laid across the front of his throat as he lay outstretched on his back. Twelve persons, chosen haphazardly and some of them weighty individuals, knelt down and grasped the pole with both hands, six side by side at each of its ends. With all pressing downwards upon the pole to keep it in position, a signal was given, and the young Japanese began his efforts to escape from beneath it. Hands pressing the floor, in a few seconds he contrived to shift his head so that the pressure was transferred to the side of his neck. Then he brought his knees beneath him, worked head and shoulders until the pole was across his nape, and two seconds later was standing erect.

A further demonstration was with Uyenishi in the upright position, on his feet, one end of the horizontal bamboo resting in the slight hollow below the Adam's Apple, the other pressed against the butt of the open right hand of a strong and heavy man, who, by a forward pressure towards the Japanese, held the pole in position. At a given signal Uyenishi commenced to walk forward from the wall against which he had been backed, and so across the room, unconcernedly driving before him his opponent, in spite of the latter's powerful efforts to maintain his place.

A full appreciation of what this feat means will be obtained by the attempt to duplicate it.

As a teacher, Uyenishi was patient in the extreme, sparing no effort to get his pupil to understand the theory and master the practice of whatever throw or movement he was demonstrating. And never would he take the least undue advantage of his own knowledge and powers. To make the pupil proficient was his sole purpose.

Ju-jutsu (*Judo*) is too commonly regarded as a collection of "foul" tricks wherein art is combined with strength and quickness to bring about a result that means the disablement of the opponent or forcing him into such a position that disablement can easily follow. Such tricks are a part of Ju-jutsu; it would not be a system of Self Defence were it otherwise; but Uyenishi was not eager to exploit this side of *Ju-jutsu*. Rather did he prefer to concentrate his attention, and the interest of his pupil, on the throws, mastery of which he held to be the first essential of *Ju-jutsu* proficiency.

For that reason the greater part of this textbook is devoted to a painstaking explanation of the several methods of bringing an opponent to the ground. In this respect it differs wholly from most other books explaining the art.

The reader is strongly recommended to turn back to Chapter IV and read carefully the opening paragraphs. When he has mastered the making of the throws that follow, he will realize that his time has been spent to greater profit than if he had devoted it to the learning of the many "trick" defences and attacks.

It is of interest to note the developments of *Ju-jutsu* in England and elsewhere. Perhaps these have not been so encouraging or so widely spread as Uyenishi had hoped.

Yet there is a greater practice of the art than appears on the surface.

Societies for the encouragement and teaching of *Ju-jutsu* have come into existence; there are numerous clubs scattered about the country which profess its teaching and practice; there are a number of private instructors. Some of the police organizations have recognized the value of the art and encourage the learning of (some part of) it among their members. A *Ju-jutsu* club has been formed at both Oxford and Cambridge Universities. Before the war perhaps the most important matches were those staged in competition for a challenge trophy presented by the Japanese ambassador to England.

The headquarters of the art in this country is the Budokwai, a club in London, open to both British and Japanese members, ladies as well as men, founded by a Mr. Koizumi, himself an expert amateur Ju-jutsuan and of high grade as a "belt" wearer. The annual Display given by members of the Budokwai shortly before Christmas was an event that no one interested in the subject could miss.

In Germany, France and other European countries existed numerous coteries for the practice and development of the art; international matches were frequently arranged. Germany had even taken the lead in establishing European *Ju-jutsu* championships, but it is not certain that these are to be taken very seriously.

One of the main principles of the Japanese art is that expert knowledge of it places the physically small and not unduly strong person (though strength and stamina are qualities having a very real value in a *Ju-jutsu* encounter, whatever may be asserted to the contrary) on a fighting equality (at least) with an opponent owning the apparent great advantages of superior bulk, weight and muscular power. The art of the Ju-jutsuan is indicated by his degree of skill which permits him to offset these advantages and obtain the victory. Yet the German *Ju-jutsu* authorities decided that the European championships should be held at certain specified weights.

To S. K. Uyenishi it was a matter of indifference whether his opponents weighed nine or sixteen stone.

Milton Keynes UK
Ingram Content Group UK Ltd.
UKHW010701220524
443011UK00002B/12